THOMAS McCLUNG
At
The Battle of Point Pleasant

Nancy Richmond

Richmond Books
Printed in North Charleston, South Carolina

Copyright 2015
All Rights Reserved

Books By Nancy Richmond

Coal Miners and Moonshiners

Appalachian Folklore

William McClung - Appalachian Frontiersman

The McClung Genealogy

Ghosts of Greenbrier County

Haunted Lewisburg, West Virginia

Grandfather Billie

Herald of Hope - The Chapel Car of Quinwood, WV

Saving Susie - An Elder Abuse Horror Story

The Battle of Lewisburg

Visit the author's web page at

nancyrichmondbooks.com

CONTENTS

1. Indian Uprising   1

2. Meeting at Williamsburg   29

3. Camp Union   53

4. Wilderness March   79

5. The Battle of Point Pleasant   105

6. Appendix   145

INDIAN UPRISING

The frontiersman moved silently through the dark and foreboding forest. A misty rain was falling, but the moisture ran down the fringes of the man's deerskin shirt and leggings and dripped onto the ground, leaving him dry and comfortable in the dampness of the gathering night.

Thomas McClung had been scouting the perimeters of his homestead, making sure that no Indian raiding parties were in the area. Finding no sign of recent activity, he made his way back to the isolated log cabin that stood on a ridge just above Muddy Creek Hollow.

What was known as the Greenbrier Territory lay on the western border of Virginia Colony, and was often invaded by small bands of Shawnee hunters during their summer forays into the valley. Thus far, the pioneer family had been spared from an attack, but were constantly on the alert for signs that one might be imminent.

Thomas had followed his younger brother William McClung from Rockbridge County into the Appalachian wilderness in 1770. There he took a 'tomahawk claim' for a large tract of land where he could build a home for his wife Nancy and their children.

At the end of the French and Indian War, the English government made treaties with the various native tribes and assured colonists that it was safe to settle in the vast unoccupied region between the east coast and the Indian territories of Ohio. But by 1774, renegade war parties had begun raiding along the border, pillaging and robbing the farms that had sprung up along the Greenbrier River and its tributaries; capturing or killing the colonists and stealing their guns, livestock and other possessions.

Satisfied that his family was not in any immediate danger, Thomas strode across the clearing that surrounded the cabin, calling to his wife to unbar the door and let him in. Stepping into the warm interior of the snug log structure, he stretched and shook himself, spraying droplets of cold rainwater on his children, who squealed and ran to the other end of the room.

"Thomas!" his wife Nancy's voice was reproachful, but her deep blue eyes sparkled with laughter. "How can I teach the children manners when their father acts like a wild animal?"

Thomas smiled down at his pretty red headed wife. Although she only came up to his shoulder, Thomas knew Nancy was the heart and soul of their family, and he would do anything in his power to please her.

"That's why I have you, wife," he teased. "To make up for all my faults." Thomas took off his rain soaked hat and shirt, and hung them above the wooden mantle to dry.

Even at the age of forty four, Thomas McClung was an impressive sight standing bare chested in the light of the flickering fire. He was well over six feet in height, with wide shoulders and a muscular torso. His jet black hair, that hung almost to his waist, was tied with a rawhide band into the traditional colonial queue. Deep set brown eyes and a square jaw gave him a rugged but handsome face that could be gentle or stern, depending upon his mood.

Thomas slipped a muslin shirt over his head, and seated himself at the rough hewn table in the corner of the room. Nancy brought him a plate of stew, and he sat talking with his family as he ate, assuring them that they had no need to fear an Indian attack for the time being. His gaze scanned the room, taking in the pleasant scene.

The frontier couple's oldest son John was almost sixteen, and considered himself the second man of the house. Alexander was a year younger, but he was just as dependable. Jane and Rachel were ten and eight, and were already a great help to their mother with the chores, and with taking care of four year old Edward, who always seemed to be into some kind of mischief.

Thomas Junior, who was only a few months old, slept peacefully in his mother's arms as she sat watching her husband eat. The other children had inherited Nancy's fair skin and red hair, but baby Thomas had his father's dark eyes, and was already sprouting a thick shock of black hair on his tiny head.

The border man pushed himself back from the table, and bedded down the fire. The five older children climbed the ladder into the loft that was their bedroom, and Thomas drew a homespun linen curtain around the corner of the cabin that contained a handmade bedstead with its straw tick mattress.

Nancy laid the sleeping baby in the

cradle that his father had made for him, which sat at the foot of the bed, then the couple retired too. Sleep was a long time coming for Thomas, however, as he fretted about the Indian uprising and the danger it presented to his family.

As a British subject, Thomas had been required by law at the age of eighteen to become part of the colonial militia. The militia was an armed force composed of every free adult male citizen of the Commonwealth of Virginia capable of bearing arms. Its primary purpose was to repel invasions and insurrections and to enforce the laws of the colony as set forth by England.

The militia was often less of a fighting unit than it was a pool of armed men who were available for service on a regional basis. If problems arose, the English government put together 'marches' made up of men from various local militias to face any threat to the colonies.

When the French and Indian War began in 1754, a formal act was passed by the British Parliament that further defined the duties of the colonial militia. It read:

"Whereas it is necessary, in the time of danger, that the militia should be well regulated and disciplined, and be it further enacted, by the authority of aforesaid, that every person shall be armed in the manner following, that is to say: Every soldier shall be furnished with a firelock well fixed, a bayonet fitted to the same, a double cartouch (cartridge) box, and three charges of powder, and will constantly appear with the same, at the time and place appointed

for muster and exercise, and shall also keep at his place of abode one pound of powder and four pounds of ball, and bring the same with him into the field when he shall be required.

And for the better training and exercising of the militia, and rendering them more serviceable, be it further enacted, that every captain shall, one in three months, and oftener if thereto required by the lieutenant or chief commanding officer in the county, muster, train and exercise his company, to be made in the months of March or April, and September or October, yearly."

Whenever Thomas had been called to serve in the militia in the past, his family had been safe in Rockbridge County while he was away. But now, he knew that they would be alone and defenseless in the wilderness if he were ordered to take part in a military march.

Wearily, Thomas decided that there was nothing he could do about the problem until it occurred, so he would wait and deal with it then. Just before dawn, he drifted off into a restless sleep.

****

The hot summer days of August passed quickly on the McClung homestead. Thomas worked his fields, hunted game in the huge stands of forest that surrounded the cabin, and fished with his sons on the banks of Muddy Creek. The long midsummer evenings provided additional hours of daylight for Thomas to sit outside on the cabin 'stoop' and sharpen his knives and tomahawk, clean his carbine rifle, and mold the lead balls that it shot.

One sultry night, just as the full August moon began to rise above the tree line, Thomas heard the sound of horses approaching. He stood in the doorway of the cabin and watched as three British soldiers, dressed in their red coats and triangular hats, rode out of the trees at the edge of the clearing.

As the men neared the cabin, Thomas could tell by their uniforms that the leader of the group was a Sargent, and the other men were privates. The officer dismounted and walked briskly toward Thomas. As he approached, a deep, menacing growl erupted from the darkness at the side of the log house.

"Citizen, call off your dog," the soldier called out to the frontiersman.

Thomas turned to look behind him, where the moonlight was clearly reflected in the eyes of an animal crouched in the shadows beside the building.

" Well, I would, but the fact is I don't have a dog," Thomas replied calmly.

The Sargent gave the frontiersman a disgusted look.

"Do you take me for a fool, man?" the officer demanded, pointing toward the sound of the growls. "If you don't have a dog, then what the hell do you call that?"

Thomas gave the irate man a slow smile, and drawled, "Well, I don't know where you fellers are from, but round these parts, we call it a wolf."

With that Thomas snapped his

fingers and a huge grey buffalo wolf padded silently out of the darkness to stand beside his master. The British officer took a step back, then guffawed loudly when Thomas motioned towards the woods and the wolf loped out of sight. The men shook hands and Thomas invited them into the cabin, where Nancy served them plates of cold turkey with bread and fresh churned butter.

While they were eating, one of the men asked Thomas how he came to have a buffalo wolf as a pet. Thomas replied that he and his sons had been fishing on Muddy Creek after a heavy rain the year before, when they saw the young wolf pup being carried down the stream by the heavy current.

Thomas had jumped into the rushing water and managed to lay hands on the cub before it was washed away. The beast had been with them ever since, and had proven itself to be a trusted guardian for the family.

"I wanted to name him Devil," Thomas told the soldiers, smirking naughtily at Nancy, "but my wife is superstitious and said it would bring bad luck to us, so I call him 'Old Scratch' instead."

The soldier dropped his head to hide a smile, and continued eating. After the hungry men finished their meal, Thomas asked the Sargent what the purpose of their visit was. News from the outside world was hard to come by for the pioneer families on the border, so the McClungs waited with interest to hear what he had to say.

The officer began by relating the events that had been taking place in the colonies for the past year. He said that the great Shawnee Indian Chief Cornstalk was stirring up the various branches of the tribe, that included the Piqua (men born of ashes), the Kiskapoke (men of war), the Mequacheke (fat men) and the Chillicothe (dwellers in a permanent home), in the hope that they would agree to declare war against the white settlers who now occupied the Greenbrier territories from the edge of Virginia Colony to the Ohio River.

Together the tribes had promised to provide one thousand warriors for the war effort. The Shawnee were renowned for their bravery in battle, and were considered to be the 'Spartans of their race'.

According to the Sargent, his militia Captain John Stuart had warned the troops about the ferocity of the Shawnee tribe, saying, "Of all the Indians, the Shawnee are the most bloody and terrible, holding all other men, Indians as well as whites, in contempt as warriors in comparison with themselves. That opinion makes them more restless and fierce than any other savages; and they have boasted that they have killed ten times as many white people as any other Indian nation."

In addition to their own warriors, the Shawnee had made treaties with the Delaware tribes, who promised to provide five hundred and fifty braves to Cornstalk. The Wyandot Nation, whose motto was 'Wyandot will not be taken alive', agreed to match that number.

The renegade natives began making raids against the settlers in the spring of 1774. They traveled through the territory at will, killing and scalping men, women and children, and burning their homes.

One war party attacked a settlement at Cedar Grove, where they killed the homesteader Walter Kelly and his servant. The other members of the family escaped, but the village was lost.

A few weeks later, the Indians confronted a group of militia under Captain John Dickenson at the mouth of the Greenbrier River. Several soldiers were wounded and one was killed.

Arbuckle's Fort had been fired on, and one man (Walter Kelly's brother) was killed before he could take shelter in the stockade. His young daughter was taken prisoner and carried off by the savages of the raiding party.

In response to the atrocities, the British authorities had issued a letter of warning to the colonial militia, telling them to expect an attack by the natives, and to prepare themselves to repel their advance.

Many of the angry backwoodsmen took the letter as declaration of war. They dubbed the conflict 'Cresaps War' in memory of a group of surveyors led by Michael Cresap that had been ambushed by Indians earlier that year.

In retaliation for the Shawnee attacks, the local militia had raided several Indian encampments, including the village of a friendly group of Mingo tribesmen, where they killed the family of Chief Logan, who was a friend of the white men. The actions of the border men further inflamed the anger of the renegade tribes toward the settlers.

Lord Dunmore, Governor of the

Virginia Colony, directed Colonel Andrew Lewis to have his soldiers build a fort on the Kanawha River as a base of operations and then to destroy all the Indian villages in the area. Lewis and his troops had complied at once.

At the same time, Major Angus McDonald led an army of four hundred men from Fort Dunmore to the Shawnee village of Wakotomica on the Muskingum River, hoping to make a treaty with their chief. However, Indian scouts warned the natives of the approaching army, and the village was deserted when the troops arrived.

In anger, McDonald ordered that the town be burned to the ground. He then returned with his men to the Shenandoah Valley.

When Governor Dunmore learned of

McDonald's failure, he called for the creation of a large expeditionary force to be used to combat the Indian threat. Dunmore himself would lead the northern regiments, or right wing, of the army, which numbered over thirteen hundred men.

The Governor then appointed Colonel Andrew Lewis to be the commander of the combined forces of the southern regulars and the militia, which would make up the left wing of the army. Altogether, the soldiers and the militia in the southern regiments would contain more than one thousand troops.

Lord Dunmore's objectives, he informed the Virginia House of Burgess, were to first make the banks of the Ohio River the seat of the war, or line of defense; and secondly to invade the Ohio wilderness.

Once there, the army would destroy the Shawnee villages on the Pickaway Plains, in the Scioto River Valley.

When the British officer finished informing the McClungs about the terrible attacks along the border, a shocked silence hung over the room for several minutes. When no one spoke, the Sargent continued.

"All of the militias in the more settled areas have already been called into service. My men and I were sent out to notify everyone living on the outskirts of the territory that there has been a call to arms.

Every able bodied man from this district must report for duty at Camp Union near Fort Savannah on the Big Levels no later than the last day of August, and must be fully outfitted for the journey, armed and ready to march."

"And what will become of our women folk and children while we are fighting in Dunmore's War?" Thomas demanded. "I won't leave my kin to fend for themselves if the Indians attack."

"Have no fear of that," replied the Sargent. "Several of the best militia companies will be chosen to stay behind and defend the territory while we march to the Ohio. Besides, the savages will be too occupied with the main force to send any raiding parties south."

Satisfied that his family would be safe, Thomas agreed to pack his gear and ride to Camp Union with all speed. He tried to avoid looking at the frightened expression on Nancy's face as he conferred with the soldiers.

The Sargent, who had been watching

the McClung's large and powerfully built oldest son, asked the boy if he would be joining the militia. John eagerly stepped forward, saying that he would be happy to accompany his father, but Nancy quickly grabbed his arm and pulled him back, telling the British officer that her son was not yet sixteen and was too young to fight.

Seeing the disappointed look on the boy's face, Thomas patted John's shoulder and told him, "Never mind, for you must become the man of the house while I am away and take care of the family and the farm."

Only slightly mollified, John followed the soldiers outside and helped them bed their horses down. The men slept on the floor of the cabin that night, and were grateful to be inside when a heavy rain fell just before dawn.

After eating the hearty breakfast that Nancy made them, the soldiers prepared to continue their trek through the mountains. Thomas gave them directions to the nearest homestead, which was several miles east of his farm.

The frontiersman asked the Sargent to tell his neighbor, Henry Dickenson, that he would ride over soon so they could make plans to travel to Camp Union together. The soldier agreed to pass on the information, and the men were almost out of sight when the Sargent wheeled his horse around and rode back toward the cabin.

"I just remembered that I have a message for you from your father," he called out to Thomas.

"My father?" Thomas replied in

surprise. "He and my mother live in Rockbridge County, not on the border."

"Well, he is in Williamsburg at the moment," the Sargent answered. "He's staying with your brother William at the old blockhouse on the Stuart homestead, and asked that you stop by there on your way to Camp Union."

Thomas expressed his thanks to the officer, and went into the cabin to tell Nancy that his parents were visiting nearby. But the look of despair that his wife gave him as he entered the room drove everything from his mind except for the desire to comfort her.

Nancy was standing beside the cabin's single window, whose shutters had been opened to let in the late summer breeze, and had heard the conversation between Thomas and the soldiers. She was nursing little Thomas, and the frontiersman wrapped his long arms around them both, holding them tightly against his chest.

Pressing her face against his rough muslin shirt, Nancy began to cry as if her heart were broken.

"Thomas, don't go," she sobbed. "There was an owl sitting on the steps when I went to fetch water this morning, and that is surely a bad omen. What will I do without you?" she wailed.

Thomas lifted her and the baby into his arms and carried them to the bed, where he sat down, holding her on his lap as if she were a child. He covered her wet face with kisses. When she finally quieted, he took her chin in his hand and turned her face up to his.

"Nancy, look around us. This is what life is meant to be. We are free, our children are free, we have our own land, and each other. I can't - I won't - let anything take that away from us. If it means I have to go and fight for that, then I will. If it means I die fighting for that, then so be it," His voice softened as he looked down at his trembling wife.

"Honey, I can't stay home and let someone else do my fighting for me. What kind of a man would I be? What kind of husband and father would I be? You and the children will be safe here, and will prosper, whether I come back or not. And that is what is important." He leaned forward to press his lips against hers.

"But don't worry, my sweet, this long hair of mine will never decorate the wigwam of some savage. Its much too purty for that."

Nancy smiled up at him through her tears, and he winked at her.

MEETING AT WILLIAMSBURG

Thomas rode along an ancient buffalo trail that meandered through the forest of white pine, chestnut and maple trees that covered Muddy Creek Mountain. His deerskin saddle bags held the few belongings that he had packed for the long march that the militia would be making to the Ohio River. His 'possibles' bag, which was the border men's name for their ammunition pouch, held his black powder and the lead balls he had made during the summer. Nancy had sewn a large deer skin duffle bag for his few personal items, and thus lightly supplied, he began his journey.

The buffalo trail eventually veered left, but the homestead of Henry Dickenson was to the right. Thomas dismounted and led his horse through the heavy underbrush of lilac and rhododendron bushes that flourished in the area until he came to the path Henry had cleared near his cabin.

Thomas shouted a loud 'Hallo' to his neighbor to let him know that his visitor was friendly, and the young man appeared in the doorway. Unlike most of the settlers in the Greenbrier territory, Henry was single. He had left his father's home in Lexington and come alone to the border to make his fortune.

Still in his early twenties, Henry had a boyish look about him, and was friendly and gregarious. He was always willing to help his neighbors, and was liked by all of the local families.

Thomas saw that Henry's horse was saddled and his bags were packed, so he knew the British troops had already stopped and given Dickenson the call to arms.

Henry went back into his cabin to finish his preparations, and Thomas followed him inside. The younger man's log home was much smaller than the one Thomas had built, and looked more like an oversized shed than a residence. Henry always agreed when anyone commented on that fact, and said he was waiting to find a wife so that he could redo the place to her wishes after they married.

Thomas asked Dickenson what he planned to do about his livestock and his crops that were not yet ready to be reaped. The young man replied that one of the older farmers in the settlement had promised that he and his two teen aged sons would take care of the place and harvest the crops in exchange for a share of everything.

    The two men led their horses to the buffalo trail and then mounted up, anxious to be on their way. When Thomas told Henry that he was going to ride north to Williamsburg to see his family before heading to Camp Union, the young man gladly agreed to accompany him. Henry was a second cousin to Abigail Dickenson Carpenter, who had married William McClung, and he was delighted to have a chance to visit with her and hear any news she might have about their relatives.

    Thomas had seven younger brothers, but he had been closest to William when they were growing up. William had been the first of the McClung brothers to venture onto the frontier, and had gone further than any other white man, to the banks of the Big

Clear Creek in the southernmost part of the territory. The homestead William chose was almost twenty miles from the closest settlement, and as he found out later, was within sight of the Midland Trail that the Shawnee used during their summer hunting trips. By 1773 the threat of an Indian attack had become so bad that William had to hide his wife and three small sons in the nearby swamp whenever he worked his fields, which he plowed with his gun on his shoulder for their protection.

    Eventually, the danger grew too great, so William and his family left their farm and retreated north to Williamsburg, a small village that was near one of the many forts that had been built along the edge of the frontier. Once there, they moved into an old blockhouse owned by the wealthy Stuart clan of Staunton, Virginia, who were cousins of William's mother Rebecca. William decided not to return to his homestead until the hostilities with the Indians had been dealt with, especially now that his wife Abigail was expecting their fourth child.

Thomas knew that William, as a member of the militia, would be riding to Camp Union to make the march to the Ohio, so he wanted to stop at the Stuart homestead not only to see his parents, but also to ask William if he wanted to join them on their ride to the Big Levels.

It took two days for Thomas and Henry to reach the Williamsburg settlement. The weather was warm and there was no rain, so their trip through the mountains was uneventful. On the evening of the second day, the men reached the edge of the property where the old blockhouse stood. It had originally been a meeting place for the militia, and was then used as a storage building by the Stuarts, but now the two story structure had been converted into a home for William and his family.

As they rode toward the log building, the riders were startled to see a Delaware Indian brave standing in the front yard. Thomas reached for his rifle, but before he could shoulder it, his father John McClung emerged from the house, and began talking with the brave. When they drew closer, Thomas realized that the 'Indian' was actually his youngest brother Charles, who was outfitted in full Delaware regalia.

"Thomas!" John McClung called to his oldest son. "I'm glad that you got my message. It's good to see you."

John McClung had been born in Ulster, Ireland in 1706, and had immigrated to America in the 1720s, but even after fifty years in the English colonies, he still spoke with a heavy Scottish accent. Like Thomas, his long black hair was pulled back into an English pony tail, but his was now liberally sprinkled with gray. After Thomas had dismounted, John gave his son a hearty bear hug, then he turned to Henry.

"And who is this strapping young man?" he asked, smiling and shaking his hand.

"Pa, this is Henry Dickenson, my neighbor, and a cousin to Abigail," Thomas replied.

"Then he is equally welcome here. Now Thomas, what do you think of your

Indian brother Charles? He has been living with the Christian Delaware tribe in Rockbridge, learning to be a scout and tracker for the militia, and they like him so much they have made him a blood brother." John rolled his eyes and laughed.

Charles turned to Thomas and smiled. Always quiet and reserved, the Indian gear seemed to suit him. And with his black hair and sun browned skin, he very much looked the part of a young Indian brave. Even so, although there was a twenty-five year age difference between the two brothers, it would have been hard to distinguish them from one another at a distance.

John led everyone into the house, where things were in a pleasant sort of disarray. William's three young boys, John,

James and Billie were running wildly though the house, romping and playing with a litter of hound puppies, who were equally occupied with chasing two large cats. Their mother Abigail and grandmother Rebecca were busily maneuvering through the disorder, putting bowls and platters of food on the long wooden table that took up most of the space in the front room.

It had been three years since Thomas had seen his mother. When she turned and caught sight of him, she gasped and ran to hug him. He picked her up and swung her around the room until she declared she was dizzy and made him put her down. Her cheeks were pink and her eyes glowed with happiness, even when she scolded him for such foolish behavior.

Rebecca was a true pioneer's wife;

strong and self reliant. She had been beautiful and well educated for a woman of her time, and had good prospects when she was young. She could have married a store clerk or clergyman or politician in one of the civilized towns on the east coast, but instead she chose the handsome young Scotch-Irish newcomer John McClung to be her husband, and she had never regretted that decision.

Together John and Rebecca had raised their family on a three hundred acre tobacco farm in what was known as the Forks area of Rockbridge County. Since there were no schools nearby, Rebecca spent several hours each day teaching her children to read and write and do sums. Now that they were grown, Rebecca did the same for her many grandchildren.

Thomas turned and smiled down at William's wife Abigail. It was obvious that she was expecting a child soon, but even so she seemed slender and somewhat fragile. She had thick blonde hair that hung in long, natural curls, and a small heart shaped face that was accentuated by her large brown eyes.

Thomas greeted his sister-in-law and gave her a gentle hug. Abigail's mother died when she was only four, and her father Joseph Carpenter had not been able to raise the little girl alone, so he brought her back to her grandparents, the Dickensons, who had taken her in. Although Abigail seemed delicate, the frontier life she lived with William had proven that she had an inner core of pure steel.

"Where is William?" Thomas

inquired of Abigail when he realized her husband had not yet appeared.

"He rode out yesterday to see your brother Samuel at his farm on Blue Sulphur Springs," she replied. "They should be back soon."

Abigail caught site of her cousin Henry, whom she had not seen since she was a child, and happily greeted him. They reminisced about the Dickenson family while she finished preparing the evening meal.

The women served broiled trout that was fresh from the nearby stream, roasted deer venison, and newly dug sweet potatoes that had been cooked into a pie, plus the hot baked bread that was a staple of the pioneer diet. The adults sat at the long table, while the boys ate sitting on the floor, which allowed them to slip pieces of meat from their plates to the dogs when their mother was not looking.

After eating, the four men went outside to smoke some of the fresh tobacco that John had brought with him from Rockbridge. Thomas asked his father what had brought him and his mother so far from their farm, to which John replied that he had agreed to help deliver supplies from Rockbridge to the militia force at Camp Union.

John was still a member of the colonial militia, although he was now too old to fight. Instead, he and the other men over fifty years of age were expected to provide horses, cattle, flour and other goods to support the war effort.

John and Rebecca, along with a few

other homesteaders, transported the supplies to the Greenbrier territory along the Great Wagon Road, which ran from Pennsylvania to the Shenandoah River Valley in Virginia and on to the headwaters of the James and New Rivers. They eventually arrived at Williamsburg, where they picked up more goods from the local farmers.

After their arrival at the Stuart farm, John sent for Thomas and Samuel in the hope that they would assist William in delivering the supplies to Camp Union, so that he and Rebecca could remain with Abigail and her children while William was on the march with the militia. Both Thomas and Henry readily agreed.

When William and Samuel had not arrived at the blockhouse by dark, it was assumed that the men had decided to bed down in the forest until morning, so the family retired for the night. The large old block house was roomy, and there were plenty of blankets for the guests, so after talking far into the night, they bid one another goodnight and went to sleep.

****

After breakfast the next morning, Charles invited Thomas and Henry to watch him shoot his Indian bow. He proudly displayed the arrows he had made himself, and after marking targets on a large pine tree behind the cabin, he demonstrated his skill with the weapon. The usually somber young man was cheerful and animated, bragging that he could loose three arrows before an enemy with a gun could take his first shot.

The other men tried their luck with the bow, but found that it took a great deal of practice to be able to control the direction of the arrow. They praised Charles for his ability, and his face glowed with pride. He revealed that he had not made the trip just to help his father with the wagons, but also because he intended to join the militia on their march to confront the Indian army at the Ohio River.

Thomas objected, saying, "But Charles, you are too young for the militia. You are not yet eighteen."

Charles replied that he would be of age by the end of the year.

"I can shoot better than most of the men I know, and none of them can beat me with a bow or a tomahawk. What difference does a few months make?" Charles argued.

"If you and Samuel and William will stand good for me, no one will even bother to ask about my age."

Thomas did not want to see his young brother involved in the battle he knew was going to take place, but he also knew that on the frontier it took more than years to change a boy into a man. Reluctantly, he agreed to take Charles with them when they left for Camp Union.

By the time the men returned to the blockhouse, William and Samuel had arrived. Samuel was Captain of the Muddy Creek Mountain militia, and had already started to the Big Levels with his men when William met them on the road. Upon learning that his parents were nearby, he sent his troops on ahead, telling them he would catch up with them at the Fort.

The four brothers greeted each other with much hand shaking and back slapping, teasing one another about how the years had changed them all, and fondly remembering past times, when they had grown up on the family farm in Rockbridge County. Many of the skills they now relied on as frontiersmen had been learned there.

The McClung brothers formed an arresting tableau. They were all tall and powerfully built, with handsome features and piercing eyes that were very similar. It would have been obvious even to a casual observer that the men were closely related.

John and Rebecca entered the room, and Samuel enveloped them both in a tight embrace, leaning down to kiss his mother on the forehead. Abigail and her boys joined the reunion, and William embraced his wife tenderly and asked about her health before being wrestled to the floor by his three rambunctious sons.

After the evening meal, the men gathered around the long table to discuss the upcoming expedition. Samuel, as an officer in the militia, had read most of the messages that had been sent by Lord Dunmore, outlining the proposed assault on the Shawnee tribes. The reports stated that the southern and northern divisions of the army would rendevous at the convergence of the Ohio and Kanawha Rivers. From there they would march on the Shawnee army, pushing them back into the Ohio territories and forcing them to sign a peace treaty. The combined colonial forces would contain nearly three thousand men, while the Indians would not be able to raise an army of more than two thousand braves.

After Samuel finished outlining the militia's strategy, everyone agreed that it was a good one. However, the other news he gave them was even more disturbing to the frontiersmen than the prospect of the upcoming militia march.

When Samuel talked with the British soldiers that were traveling through the area, sounding the call to arms, they told him that the British legislature had recently passed laws forbidding any of the thirteen colonies from buying goods from any country except England. In addition to those restrictions, the colonists would now have to pay high taxes on those goods.

The House of Burgess, a governing body made up of representatives from each of the colonies, refused to adopt the new measures, so England stationed an army of seven thousand soldiers in the cities along the coast to enforce the laws. In protest, a group of colonists, dressed as Indians, boarded an English ship in the Boston harbor and dumped a shipment of tea into the bay. Now the Americans were waiting to learn what the reaction of the English Parliament would be.

When Samuel finished speaking, there was a stunned silence in the room. Then Thomas leaped to his feet and struck his fist against the table.

"By God," he cried, " England does not give us anything in this country. What we don't do ourselves, doesn't get done. If we are men, we won't allow it. It is time the British Lords learn that we are no longer their whipping boys."

Like most of the Scotch-Irish who migrated to America in the 1700s, the McClungs were a strong and proud family. Their ancestors had lived on the border between Scotland and England, where they constantly made war between the clans, and where raiding was a way of life.

When the descendants of those independent people came to America, they were treated with contempt by the wealthy British landowners, and were often beaten from the towns. Many escaped onto the frontier, taking nothing with them but their courage, axes to build homes, and firearms to defend themselves.

During the French and Indian War, Britain had done little to protect the border families, and the homesteaders quickly learned it was up to them to take care of themselves. They had come to despise English authority. They believed that their fate was in their own hands, and lived accordingly.

William McClung reacted with the same ferocity as Thomas to the news, declaring "If it is a fight the British want, then they will have one. No man can tell me what I can do on my own land."

The discussion continued into the early hours of the morning.

At last John declared that although his spirit was willing, his flesh was old, and he needed to rest before taking on the whole of the British army. Everyone laughed. After agreeing to wait and see how the English reacted to the Boston Tea Party before passing judgment on them, they all went to bed.

CAMP UNION

At dawn on the morning of August 25, 1774, the four McClung brothers and Henry Dickenson left Williamsburg for Camp Union, where the band of rugged frontiersmen would join the colonial forces of Colonel Andrew Lewis. Because the old Indians trails that led to the Big Levels were narrow and uneven, wagons could not be used to transport the army supplies that John McClung had collected, so they had to be carried by pack horses. Although that slowed the progress of the convoy considerably, the men were all in good spirits.

Thomas had managed to talk Charles into exchanging his Indian garb for a deerskin shirt and leggings. However, he refused to give up his moccasins for the more popular knee high boots of tanned animal hide that the other men wore.

The game trail wound its way through some of the best hunting grounds in the territory, and it was not unusual for the group to encounter a mother bear and her cubs or a herd of deer on the path, which had to be chased off before they could continue on their way. The men kept a close watch for signs of renegade Indians, and posted a sentry when they camped each night, but they saw no evidence that anyone had traveled the trail recently.

By the time the frontiersmen reached the outskirts of Camp Union, which was near Fort Savannah, there were nearly a thousand men camped in and around the blockhouse and stockade. The Fort had been built in 1755 at the site of two mountain springs which provided fresh water for the soldiers who were stationed there.

The air was filled with the sounds of men's voices, the neighing of horses, the lowing of cattle, and the rattle of drums. The noises seemed disruptive and out of place in the heart of the wilderness.

Captain Samuel McClung bid his brothers goodby and went in search of the chief quarter-master to deliver the supplies. In the meantime, the other men located an unoccupied area at the edge of the forest to set up their campsite before reporting for duty to one of the officers.

Division headquarters was located in the Barracks, a large two story wooden building that had been built to house soldiers a few years earlier. Colonel Andrew Lewis was the Commander in charge of the army, and second in command was his brother Charles Lewis. Besides the Augusta County Regiment, the Botetourt County Regiment and the Fincastle County Battalion, there were several independent companies. These included the Culpeper Minute Men, The Dunmore County Volunteers, The Bedford County Riflemen and the Kentucky Volunteers.

Because the Muddy Creek settlement was located in a section of Botetourt County that did not have a regular militia company, Thomas, William and Henry were assigned to the Bedford Riflemen in the Botetourt Regiment, which was commanded by Colonel Lewis. Samuel, who was the Captain of the local militia at Blue Sulphur

Springs, was given command of that company, and Charles was assigned to his unit. It was one of the militia groups that was ordered to stay behind to protect the homesteaders in the event that the Indians won the upcoming battle. Samuel and Charles were both disappointed not to be going with the army, but Thomas and William were relieved to know that their families would be safe should they not return from the march.

The army at Camp Union was made up of the most remarkable body of men that had ever been assembled on the American frontier. Many of the troops had been with General George Washington at the surrender of Fort Necessity, some had been with Braddock at the Battle of Monongahela, and others had been with Forbes at the capture of

Fort Du Quesne. Nearly all of them had been engaged in the Border Wars. Hence, the men gathered at the Camp were not only schooled in British and Colonial Army military tactics, they were familiar with the methods of Indian warfare as well.

The militiamen did not have regular uniforms as such, although a few of the colonial officers wore regulation military attire. The remainder of the men were almost universally clad in the accepted garb of the border. They wore hunting shirts with leather leggings, breeches of tanned animal skins, and caps made from the carcasses of wild animals or knit from wool. Each man carried the long flint-lock rifle, or English musket, with bullet pouches and quaintly carved powder horns, as well as tomahawks and hunting knives. They were seasoned fighters and defenders of their homesteads, Border Rangers, who were now ready to take the offensive against the enemy.

The camp was in a state of organized chaos, and was still awaiting the arrival of several other regiments and additional supplies. The men mingled with one another while they waited to begin the march, often running into friends or family members who were assigned to other units.

The Lewis Spring, which had been discovered by Andrew Lewis years earlier, was located near Fort Savannah and was the main water source for the area. Many of the soldiers took the opportunity to bathe and wash their clothes at the spring before beginning the long trek through the wilderness, and the McClung brothers were among those who did. While they were bathing, Charles noticed a long, wicked looking scar on Samuel's abdomen, and asked about the source of the wound. Samuel replied that he had gotten separated from his men during a Shawnee raid and four or five of the braves chased him into the forest. They were aware, although Samuel was not, that there was a steep cliff at the end of the trail, with a rocky creek at the bottom of a twenty foot drop.

The Indians were confident that they would be able to catch the white man when he reached the cliff, since it was a distance of at least fifteen feet to the other side of the chasm, a leap that no man could make. So, rather than shoot him as he ran, the braves allowed Samuel to try and escape, laughing and joking about how he would either fall to his death or be captured.

"To make a long story short," Samuel said, smiling at Charles, "when I saw that cliff ahead I did not even have time to think about it, I just jumped as hard as I could. The next thing I knew I was lying on the other bank. Let me tell you, those Indians began howling and screaming, and then they started shooting. One ball hit me here, near the groin, but I managed to get up and took off running again."

"Another one fired," Samuel continued, "and damned if he didn't shoot the queue right off of my head. It took me a year to grow that hair back, and I have often wondered if they came across the creek to find it and take it back to their village as proof that they killed me."

Charles, who had never been in any kind of battle, was throughly impressed. He hoped he would be as brave and as lucky as Samuel had been if he was ever in a similar situation.

****

The southern army languished at Camp Union, waiting for enough supplies to be accumulated for the army to begin the long march to the Ohio River. The men cleaned their equipment or practiced drills during the day, and every evening huge bonfires were built and rations were handed out so that the men could prepare their supper.

There was a small company of British army regulars assigned to the nearby fort who sometimes left the stockade to mingle with the militiamen. The recent actions of the English Crown against the colonies had caused a good deal of friction between the Virginians and the English troops stationed in America, which incited the British soldiers to occasionally make snide remarks about the clothing and weaponry of the colonial army. The jibes and taunts of the Englishmen that once might have been taken as a joke by the militia were now considered to be insults, especially since the foppish British soldiers looked equally strange to the eyes of the frontiersmen. One custom of English military attire that was a constant source of fun to the rugged mountain men was the practice of hair powdering. Since 1748, the male population in England and many of the wealthy colonial landowners in America had adopted the fad of wearing large powdered wigs. The commanders of the Royal army all wore the heavy, cumbersome hair coverings, which itched constantly and were full of bugs, but wigs were not practical for the regular troops. Instead, the rank and file of the military tied their hair back into a queue, and each soldier was issued a half a pound of flour and tallow per week to with which to powder their hair. Soldiers were required to appear freshly powdered at all times, whether in camp, on parade or in battle, and were punished if they did not do so.

On the last night of August, Thomas, William and Henry were squatting at their campfire, holding strips of bacon that had been issued to them for their supper over the open flames. Like most of the militia, they used the sharp tips of their bayonets as skewers on which to cook their food. Englishmen considered this habit to be a misuse of the firearms provided to the colonials by the Crown. As a group of British regulars walked past the McClung camp, the border men heard their Lieutenant snicker.

"Little wonder that Lord Dunmore considers the southern army to be merely 'a body of men' instead of a fighting force," the Lieutenant said loudly. "Dunmore says that their officers are incapable of imposing any order or discipline among them because the men are impressed from their earliest infancy with sentiments and habits very different from those acquired by persons of a similar condition in England. He says that they are not much less savage than the Indians."

The English soldiers laughed and started to pass by, but stopped when Thomas leaned his musket against a nearby tree and stood up, blocking their way.

Towering above the British regulars, Thomas winked at his companions and said with a grin "Well, at least us 'savages' know enough to put our flour on our bacon instead of on our heads."

Outraged, the offended British officer lifted his gun and aimed it point blank at Thomas. But before he could even pull back the hammer, Thomas hit the man in the face, knocking him to the ground. Wrenching the Lieutenant's weapon from his hands, he turned it on the fallen man.

Without taking his eyes off his opponent, Thomas addressed the dazed Englishman's companions, saying "Best take your hot headed friend back to the Fort, before something bad happens to him."

The men helped their Lieutenant to his feet and led him in the direction of the stockade. One soldier reached for the gun that Thomas was still holding, but the look in McClung's eyes made him drop his hand.

As the British regulars departed, helping to support their still incapacitated commander, the large crowd of colonial militia that had witnessed the encounter laughed and clapped one another on the back, loudly declaring that the British Lieutenant had only gotten what he had been asking for.

Thomas smiled at them and said "Well, boys, that's about the least work I ever had to do to get myself a new gun."

Although Thomas expected to hear

something about the incident the next day, no report was ever filed, and he did indeed have a new 'Pennsylvania rifle' to carry into the upcoming battle.

****

The hot, hazy days of August gave way to cooler, wetter September ones, and still the militia did not have enough supplies to make the 160 mile march through the mountains. The border men spent their days practicing with their guns and tomahawks in anticipation of the fighting to come. Every evening around the camp fires, there was talk of the upcoming conflict, and the more experienced soldiers exchanged information on the best way to fight the renegade natives.

The Indians, all of the frontiersmen

agreed, were not an enemy to be taken lightly. The tribes were constantly at war with one another, and the braves had developed their own tactics and strategies for battle.

Raiding parties almost always traveled and fought in groups of no more than twenty five men. The chiefs dressed in the same garb as the other braves, making it difficult to pick off the leaders of an assault. In battle, most warriors wore only a loincloth, leggings and moccasins. A few sometimes wore hunting shirts like the Virginians, allowing them to get closer to their adversaries. With eagle feathers or porcupine quills woven into their long hair, and garishly painted faces, they presented a terrifying foe to their enemies.

The Indians carried whatever kind of

firearms they could lay their hands on, including muskets, rifles, and fusils (small muskets that were mainly used for hunting.) Most preferred the older smoothbore guns, which were more accurate at close range. The primary weapon of the warriors, however, was the bow and arrow. The bows were easy to carry and silent when used. They were from four to six feet in length, and had an average range of 100 feet, which was more than twice the range of a smoothbore musket.

For close encounters, braves used large hunting knives and tomahawks. Many carried war clubs, which were fashioned out of hardwood and carved with a large spike on one side, which could kill a man with a single blow.

James Smith, who had fought in the

French and Indian War and had lived with the Mingo tribe for many years, warned the militia that anyone who was new at Indian warfare might see the way the natives made frequent retreats during an encounter as cowardly.

In reality, he said, the retreats were part of a much practiced tactic that the braves learned in combat training from the time they were young. Warriors would make a loosely formed line a mile wide, and move through the forest, with every man following the leader on the right end of the line.

Eventually, the braves made a wide circle around the enemy, from which it was almost impossible to escape. When the opposing forces moved forward, the Indians in the front would pull back, but at the same time, those in the rear would close in.

Thus, snakelike, the Indian line could maneuver easily, darting in and out until they had killed or captured all of the men in the circle. They were, Smith concluded, the 'best disciplined troops in the known world' in forested terrain.

Captain John Stuart, leader of one of the Botetourt companies, agreed with Smith, saying, "None will suppose we had a contemptible enemy who has any knowledge of the exploits performed by them."

Although the majority of the more experienced frontiersmen were accustomed to the Indian way of fighting, many of the young men who were new to the militia were surprised to learn that the 'wild men of the forest' used such sophisticated fighting techniques, and gained a greater respect for the army that they were about to confront.

****

On September 6th, the Augusta Regiment and part of the Botetourt Regiment, led by Colonel Charles Lewis, had garnered enough men and supplies to move out. The troops made formation and headed into the wilderness. The militia, except for officers, would make the march on foot.

Because the trails were too narrow and uneven to support the use of wagons, the army took with them five hundred pack horses, which carried 54,000 pounds of flour and ammunition. In addition, a herd of over one hundred cattle followed at the rear of the march, to be used as food during the trip.

The departure of the regiments left a shortage of supplies at Camp Union, but the quarter master made arrangements for more cattle and flour to be delivered within a week, so the Botetourt militiamen readied themselves for their own departure.

Several days later an additional supply of goods arrived, in the form of another 80,000 pounds of flour and several hundred more beef cattle. One of the men making the delivery also brought disturbing news to the frontiersman.

According to the drover, the English government had responded to the Boston Tea Party by passing 'The Coercive Acts' against Massachusetts and the colonies. The Acts, intended to punish Boston, consisted of four parts. They were:

1. The Boston Port Act - The Boston Ports

were closed until the damages from the Boston Tea Party were repaid to England.

2. The Massachusetts Government Act - Democratic town meetings were restricted and the British Governor's Council took over as the new governing body.

3. The Administration of Government Act - All British Officials in Massachusetts were immune from criminal prosecution.

4. The Quartering Act - Colonists were required to provide housing and food for all British troops, even if they had to be kept in private homes.

The Acts had the opposite effect on the colonists than those anticipated by King George III. On September 5th, delegates of twelve of the thirteen colonies met at Carpenters Hall in Philadelphia in the first meeting of a new organization called The

Continental Congress. The purpose of the Congress was to consider their options on what they dubbed The Intolerable Acts. Their first decision was to enact a boycott of all British trade in the colonies.

The meeting was still in progress when the supply transport left Lexington, so no one knew what the final outcome of the Continental Congress would be. The reaction to the news on the colonial militia was electric. Word of the Intolerable Acts spread like wildfire through Camp Union, with the men declaring unanimously that the Acts were tantamount to a declaration of War by England. The camp fires around the fort burned throughout the night, as men angrily decried the many injustices of British rule, and voiced their intentions to rebel against them if need be.

On Sunday, September 11th, the Botetourt Regiments under Colonel Andrew Lewis were informed that they would be leaving the next morning to rendevous with the Northern Army at the confluence of the Ohio and Kanawha Rivers. Thomas, Henry and William rapidly began packing their belongings and preparing for the march, which would begin at noon on the following day. Soldiers rushed about making ready for the expedition, which would include over five hundred men, and numerous pack horses that would be carrying 18,000 pounds of flour and a large amount of ammunition. The cattle herd that was being taken would follow the main force of men and horses, since it would travel more slowly so the animals could graze along the way.

As the sun began sinking beneath the

tree line, Thomas and William entered the forest at the edge of the camp, looking for firewood. Thomas impulsively climbed to the top of a small ridge, and stood watching the bustle in the camp below.

After a moment, William followed Thomas through the heavy brush that grew on the forest floor, climbing to the rocky outcrop on the summit of the ridge to stand silently beside his older brother. The sky darkened, and in the distance, the light from many campfires began to dot the landscape.

"I reckon we had better take a good look at this place tonight," Thomas said to William without turning around. "It might be a long time before we get this close to home again."

WILDERNESS MARCH

Monday, September 12: It was a hot and cloudless day, and the men of the Botetourt Regiment, headed by Colonel Lewis, were anxious to start on the long march that would take them to the intersection of the Kanawha and Ohio Rivers over 150 miles away.

The unit's clergyman held a 'Divine Service' at noon, praying for a successful journey, and the long cavalcade left Camp Union in an orderly fashion. The men crossed Muddy Creek Mountain, and at the end of the day made camp near Blue Sulphur Springs, which was well known for its hot sulphur water that was reputed to cure the ailments of those who bathed in it.

The route ran wholly through a

trackless forest, and the army climbed tall cliffs or wound its way down dangerous slopes, ascending and descending the lofty summits of the Appalachian Mountains.

Tuesday, September 13: The march resumed, and the regiment made good time, covering eleven miles. Along the way they passed Hamilton's Plantation and Jackson's Clearing. Much of the area had been devastated by Indian attacks, and by a recent fire which had destroyed most of the trees and foliage which would have given the militia cover when they made camp.

Eventually, they halted along a branch of Muddy Creek, an area that had the reputation of being 'a bad place for both food and good water'. It was near Green Sulphur Springs, another of the many hot springs that dotted the Greenbrier landscape.

Wednesday, September 14: After marching several miles, the militia crossed Meadow Creek, a tributary of Gauley River, and later crossed over Walker's Creek, a tributary of New River, where they decided to make camp.

Thursday, September 15: The regiment reached Buffalo Spring Lick, where they came across the trail of the Augusta Regiment, and followed it to Buffalo Fork, which flows into Meadow River, where they halted for the night.

Friday, September 16: The march resumed after being delayed when Captain McClennahan and Captain Henry Pauling arrived at the camp with their companies, which had been left behind to bring up some beef cattle which were lost. There were several reports of Indian activity in the area, so the firing of guns was forbidden in an effort to keep their location secure. Scouts were sent out in advance of the militia to keep watch for war parties. The regiment made good time, and camped in the Sewell Mountain district.

Saturday, September 17: The men broke camp just after sunrise and headed west over Chestnut Hill and crossed the Great Laurel Creek at 'The Warrior's Ford'. Later they crossed Little Laurel Creek and passed Mann's Hunting Camp on Mann's Creek, which is an eastern branch of New River, before stopping for the night.

Sunday, September 18: The march began early and the men traveled twelve miles over broken ridges that were covered by a chestnut forest, and camped at Laurel Run near Shade Creek, a tributary of Mill

Creek. Several scouts reported light movement by Indians in the area.

Monday, September 19: It was a day of alternate rain and sunshine. Early that morning the men began the ascent of Gauley Mountain. Colonel Lewis made the decision to take a different path than that of his advance column, and traveled over the crest of the mountain and down to the head of Rich Creek, which was a southern tributary of Gauley River. The route was rough and dangerous, with the militia traveling no more than six miles before making camp at the mouth of Rich Creek.

After rations had been dispersed and the men had eaten, William McClung and Henry Dickenson were told to leave camp at dawn to scout the mountains ahead of the regiment. They agreed, and made an early start the following morning. They moved quickly and silently through the mountains, searching for any signs that Indians had passed that way recently.

The men did not build a fire at dark, but ate the 'hard tack' bread and cold bacon they had brought with them. The next two days passed uneventfully, and on the third morning away from camp the men decided to retrace their steps and rejoin the militia.

But before the could do so, they saw movement in the forest, and a few moments later their camp was surrounded by a Shawnee war party. The two soldiers were excellent woodsmen, and had left no tracks or signs of their presence around the thicket where they had spent the night, so the Indians were completely unaware of their presence.

William and Henry lay unmoving under the heavy brush until dark, then they slowly slipped into the night, making their way back toward the militia just ahead of the Indians. The men had run out of supplies the day before, and dared not shoot any game they came across, for fear of alerting the war party of their presence.

Just before dawn, the scouts stumbled upon the hiding place of a small fawn whose mother had been killed by the war party. Knowing that it could not survive alone, William killed the fawn, and the famished men ate some of the meat raw. Then William quickly skinned the animal, rolling up the hide and placing it in his possibles bag.

Henry asked William what he wanted with such a small skin, since it was not big enough to be made into a shirt or even into a pair of moccasins.

William replied, "I am taking it home to Abigail as a gift. The binding of our family Bible is worn out, and this will make a beautiful cover for it."

The men made their way back to the regiment without any further trouble, where they reported the raiding party to their commander and rejoined their unit.

Tuesday, September 20: Before resuming the march, the company captains did an inspection of arms, then the men continued down Rich Creek for about five miles until they reached the banks of the Gauley River. The only place they could cross was over a 'stony, ugly ford' that was about 100 yards wide. The regiment then made camp on Bell Creek, having marched over eleven miles that day.

Wednesday, September 21: The army proceeded up Lick Creek for five miles, passed the divide, and moved on to Kelly's Creek, which was thick with laurel for two miles. When the western slopes became lower, the valley widened out, and was overgrown with tulip, maple, pawpaw, leatherwood and peavine.

As the troops moved across the valley floor, buffalo grass began to appear, and sweet gum. Then the ground dropped lower and the Great Kanawha River, two hundred yards wide, could be seen. It was the site of the settlement of Walter Kelly, who had been killed in a raid earlier that year. The regiment continued on to Cabin Creek, where they stopped for the night.

Thursday, September 22: The march

continued down the north side of the river. By noon the militia arrived at the mouth of the Elk River, where they met with the Augusta Regiment which had left Camp Union on September 2nd. Men from both regiments were assigned to build a store house and make canoes for transporting supplies down the Great Kanawha.

Henry Dickenson helped with the construction of the store house, while Thomas and William, who were familiar with boat building, worked with the men making canoes.

Friday, September 23: The militia stayed at the camp site, continuing their work details. Those selected for scouting duty reported at dawn for their instructions before leaving the grounds. All of the tools in the camp were put into order before being packed into the canoes.

Saturday, September 24: Pack horses were sent back to Camp Union for more flour. A court martial was held, trying Timothy Fitzpatrick for stealing a gun. He was acquitted of the charge and allowed to rejoin his unit. Provisions and ammunition were deposited in a magazine, or storage unit, which had been built for that purpose.

Because they were nearing Shawnee territory, three scouts were sent up the Elk River toward Pocatalico, three more were sent across the Kanawha to Coal River, and more were sent down the Kanawha on the north side. A church service was held for the men at noon, after which they returned to their building details.

Sunday, September 25: James Mooney, one of the scouts that had been sent over the Kanawha to Coal River, returned and reported that four miles below the mouth of the Elk, he had discovered the tracks of three horses. Only one of the horses was shod. He had also found two moccasin tracks that had passed him in the night, and went on toward the river. Scouts were sent to the mouth of the Kanawha, where they launched their canoes and went down the river. Another Divine Service was held, which all the men attended, and afterward participated in a good discourse.

Monday, September 26: Following Reveille, several orders were read to the militia by the head of each company. One stated that all men working on the building projects were exempted from guard duty. Another prohibited the miscellaneous firing of guns in and around the camp.

Tuesday, September 27: A review of the Botetourt Regiment, which included the Fincastle and Culpeper men, was held. There were 523 men accounted for. When added to the Augusta Regiment numbers, there were over 1,000 men present and accounted for, exclusive of the sick and those in service or command.

Wednesday, September 28: Scouts from Coal River returned and reported that they had discovered an encampment where fifteen Indians had rested. Captain Arbuckle and his scouts were ordered out after them, but failed to catch up with the war party. Sulters, men who followed the army and sold provisions to the soldiers, had been providing liquor to the militia, which resulted in confusion in the camp and made it necessary to prohibit any further alcohol sales other than on the orders of the Captains. Neither was any more than the supply already in camp to be allowed.

Thursday, September 29: James Fowler, one of the scouts which left on the 25th for the mouth of the Great Kanawha, returned. He reported that when he and his fellow scouts were within fifteen miles of the mouth of the river, they saw two great fires on its banks, and that on their making a noise these were immediately put out. He also reported that on their return up the river in the canoe they observed five Indians with three horses riding down the trail beside the river.

Friday, September 30: The militia drums were beat at daybreak. The fleet of twenty seven canoes which had been constructed were taken one and a half miles up Elk River, where the water was a hundred yards wide and where there was a ford. It was 'dead still' running water. The cattle and pack horses were driven over, and there the army crossed the river and made a new camp on the level plain below the mouth of the Elk.

Saturday, October 1: A heavy and incessant rain fell all through the day and night. As a result, the army remained in the camp, and the men huddled under hastily erected canvas tarps, struggling to keep their camp fires from being put out by the driving rain. Now that they were only a few days from the Ohio River and the looming battle, the mood of the militia became more somber.

As the men of the Botetourt Rifle Company ate their ration of bread and beef, one of the younger men asked if the horror stories he had heard about Old Shawnee Town on the Pickaway Plains were true.

Conversation abruptly stopped around the campfire, and the majority of the men seemed to be frozen in place. Finally, Thomas McClung set his plate on the ground beside him and addressed the group.

"I know one of the few white men who was ever taken as a prisoner to Old Shawnee Town and lived to tell the tale. He is an honest man, and I believe everything he told me about the place."

Thomas stood up, pacing back and forth in front of the fire as he spoke. "Young George See was captured by the Shawnee in 1763. He was just a lad, not more than six years old. His family and most of the other settlers in the village were killed, but about twenty men, women and children were taken captive. They were marched through the forest by the Shawnee, beaten and kicked and denied any food for days."

"When they reached the outskirts of Old Shawnee Town," Thomas continued, "George saw four ancient looking squaws waiting to greet the warriors. They were the holy women of the tribe, and they had red paint all around their mouths, so that it seemed as if they had been drinking blood. Those old women looked at all of the prisoners, and picked out four strong men who were to be killed, so that the warriors could eat their hearts and livers raw according to tribal ritual. The men were killed and scalped, and their bodies taken away to be prepared for the sacrifice."

" George told me that as soon as they entered the town, he could see a seven foot wide and one hundred foot long gauntlet, which some of the captives were picked to run while being whipped, kicked and spit on by the villagers. If they survived the ordeal, they would be adopted into the tribe."

"At the other end of the encampment there was a wide field that the Indians called 'the burning ground' where settlers were burned alive. There were skulls and other human bones scattered among the ashes around the pole. In the center of the camp was a brightly decorated wigwam, which contained the scalps of hundreds of homesteaders that had been taken by the Shawnee war parties in the years since white men first came to this land."

Thomas concluded his tale, saying "I

reckon you don't get no closer to hell on earth than that."

One of the soldiers at the edge of the campfire spoke up. "Well then, I guess it would be better to die on the battlefield than to be taken captive by the Shawnees."

"No, your wrong," Thomas corrected him. "It would be better to win the fight and then go home." With that the frontiersman turned and walked out into the night.

Saturday, October 2: Early in the morning the army formed up to march down the north side of the Great Kanawha River. Captain John Lewis, commander of the Botetourt Company, led the advance.

The left column was formed by the Botetourt troops. The Augusta troops made up the right column. Both lines contained 100 men each. The pack horses and the beef cattle were placed in the center of the two columns.

The order to march was given, and the army began to move, covering twelve miles that day. They made camp at dusk along the mouth of Coal River.

Monday, October 3: The march continued and in the afternoon the army traveled seven miles and then crossed the Pocatalico River. After continuing another mile and fording a small stream, the militia made camp for the night.

Tuesday, October 4: The men resumed their march through the wilderness shortly after dawn and passed through the narrows at Red House Shoals, where many large masses of rock, the height of which exceeded the base, stood in a line.

The troops crossed the area known as

Fallen Timber, where the hills were swept as bare as a farmer's field. Eventually, they camped two miles below the mouth of Hurricane Creek.

Wednesday, October 5: The militia broke camp early in the morning; Buffalo Creek was crossed and later in the day Eighteen Mile Creek was forded. After marching twelve miles, the men made an encampment two miles below the mouth of Thirteen-mile Creek.

Thursday, October 6: The men broke camp before dawn, hoping to make the mouth of the Kanawha River that day. Early in the morning Ten-mile Creek was crossed, as were Upper and Lower Debby Creeks shortly after.

The Eight-mile and Three-mile Creeks were forded before noon, and late in the afternoon the army crossed over Crooked Creek.

After marching eleven miles, the men came to the junction of the Great Kanawha River and the Ohio River. The land between the two bodies of water made a wide triangle, and to the weary men, it was a breath taking scene.

The trees of the surrounding forest were magnificent in their autumn colors. The Ohio River was as wide and placid as a lake, and the Kanawha resembled an estuary.

Delighted with the glorious view, the men named their campsite 'Point Pleasant'. The area seemed well fortified against an enemy attack, and the soldiers felt certain that their large force of men would instill terror into any of the Indian tribes that resided along the Ohio River should they venture upon the camp.

Colonel Lewis expected to join with Lord Dunmore's army at the 'Point', and told the troops that they would be staying in the encampment until the Northern Army arrived.

What Lewis did not know was that, after making better time than they had anticipated, Lord Dunmore had changed his plans and had led the Northern Army to the mouth of the Hocking River, where he had ordered them to build a fort.

Dunmore deployed scouts to Point Pleasant to give Colonel Lewis a message that provided his present location and his intentions to travel into Ohio. The post instructed Lewis to immediately bring his militia to the Hocking River Camp, from whence they would continue together to the

Pickaway Plains, where the Shawnee Towns were located. However, Lord Dunmore's men reached the Point several days before the arrival of the Southern Army, and rather than waiting for the militia to reach the rendevous area, they carved a message into a large hollow tree at the edge of the forest, which stated that there was a post for Colonel Lewis hidden inside the tree. The scouts then returned to the Northern Army camp.

Soon after they reached the Point, one of the militiamen of the Southern Army found the message and the post, which he delivered to Colonel Lewis. The change of plans angered Lewis and the other officers, who felt that Lord Dunmore was being reckless. Not only had he chosen a vague location in the middle of the unexplored wilderness for them to meet, the new meeting place was also in the heart of Indian territory, and was yet another fifty mile march from Point Pleasant.

Friday, October 7: Instead of preparing the men to march as he had been ordered to do, Colonel Lewis sent his own scouts to deliver a message to Lord Dunmore, telling him that some of his men had not yet arrived at the Point and that he must wait for them before breaking camp. The message also stated that the pack horses and cattle that accompanied his army were exhausted, and would require several days of rest before being able to resume travel.

Saturday, October 8: The militiamen awaited orders to begin the march that would finally unite the left and right divisions of the army. The camp remained quiet, and the weather was fair.

Sunday, October 9: Scouting parties reported to Colonel Lewis that no enemies had been sighted within fifteen miles of the camp. After hearing a good sermon, which was preached by the company clergyman, Rev. Terry, the militia went to repose.

THE BATTLE OF POINT PLEASANT

Indian scouts commanded by Chief Cornstalk had been following both the Northern and Southern Armies since they began their march toward the Ohio River two months earlier. Cornstalk had fewer men at his disposal than either of the colonial forces, so he knew that it would be best if his braves attacked before the armies combined.

Cornstalk believed that if the Southern Army was destroyed before it crossed the river, then the Northern Army could be fired upon from the hills above the valley of the Pickaway Plains, causing them to either flee or surrender.

In his bark council house in the Scioto Valley, Cornstalk consulted with the Shaman, the holy man of the tribe, who prophesied that the Indians would have a victory if they attacked the militia being led by Colonel Lewis while they were camped on the point of land that jutted out between the waterways of the Ohio and Kanawha Rivers, which the Indians called 'Tu-Endie-Wei'. Cornstalk and the Shaman left the council house and announced to the waiting braves that they would leave at daybreak to begin the attack, and the warriors began to cheer and brandish their weapons.

The Shaman carried a small carved figure of a Shawnee warrior holding a bow to the center of the village, and placed it on the top of the war post. The Indian drums began to beat the battle cadence as the warriors sang and danced around the war post, which they attacked with their tomahawks to show their prowess as fighters.

Next, the Shaman ceremoniously presented Chief Cornstalk with an ancient tomahawk, a relic of the tribe. Then he awarded headdresses made of hawk feathers to the braves who had been chosen to be leaders in the battle.

Just before dawn the following morning, the war party began the trek to Point Pleasant, traveling along the Scioto Trail. The Shaman accompanied them, carrying the tribal beeson, a leather bag containing holy objects that would be carried into battle, the same way that the army carried military flags.

By October 9th, Cornstalk's forces had set up a base on a heavily wooded ridge across the Ohio River from the camp of the Southern Army. They spent the day making rafts to traverse the river, and by the light of the autumn moon, the braves began crossing the Ohio. After reaching the southern shore, the Indians shared a ritual meal of deer meat. Before the meat was consumed, the Shaman studied each piece, searching for signs of victory in the upcoming attack.

Then the braves dressed for battle and slept sitting upright against the forest trees, in case they were unexpectedly accosted by enemy troops. An hour before dawn, the Shawnee left their campsite and headed toward Oldtown Creek, which led to Tu-Endie-Wei. The route would take them through the bottom lands on the eastern banks of the Ohio River.

Cornstalk felt that the Southern Army had unwittingly trapped itself within the boundaries of the surrounding landscape. Two sides of the Point were the waterways of the Kanawha and the Ohio Rivers, and the tents of the militia were set up in a long line along the shore of each river. The third boundary was a steep ridge that lay east of Crooked Creek. It was over two hundred feet high and nearly vertical, forming an almost impassable barrier. Cornstalk's plan was to have his warriors attack the camp exactly at daybreak, and force all the men they could not kill into the Ohio and Kanawha Rivers, where they could be held at bay until they became exhausted and drowned.

On the morning of Monday, October 10th, the encampment at Point Pleasant was guarded by a dozen sentries along a half mile line. Behind the lines were the tents of the sleeping army and the herds of cattle and horses that had made the march through the wilderness with them.

In a stroke of fate, a few of the militiamen decided to rise before dawn in order to make an expedition into the forest to hunt for turkey and deer. Two of the men, Joseph Hughey and James Mooney, made their way towards a hill a few miles north of the camp. It was the same direction from which the Indians were advancing toward the army, hoping to form a line and cut off any escape by the Virginians after they began their attack.

The militiamen reached the top of the ridge just as the sun rose over the mountains, and the sight that it revealed to them was horrific. They saw, as Mooney said later, about five acres of land covered with Indians as thick as one could stand beside another.

A dozen shots rang out from the Indian horde, and Hughey was killed instantly. Mooney turned and ran back toward the encampment with all speed, and reported what he had seen. Colonel Lewis ordered that the drums sound the alarm for the camp, which they did by beating their battle cadence 'To Arms'.

Thomas McClung woke to the throbbing of the militia drums, and was instantly awake and aware of what the sound heralded. Adrenaline rushed through his veins, and he rolled out of his blankets and got to his feet. Within a minute he had pulled his deerskin shirt over his head, donned his knee high leather boots, grabbed his weapons, and headed out to join the fight.

Colonel Lewis ordered his brother, Charles, to take command of the Augusta troops, which included the companies under Captains Dickenson, Harrison, Wilson, Lewis and Lockridge, that made up the First Division. Colonel Fleming took charge of the Botetourt, Bedford and Fincastle troops, whose companies, headed by Captains Stuart, Buford, Love, Shelby, and Russell, made up the Second Division. The men formed columns and began an orderly march into the wilderness to confront the war party.

Thomas made his way to the Second Division, and fell into step beside his brother William. They did not speak as the militia retraced the route Hughey and Mooney had taken just an hour earlier.

By six thirty, Cornstalk and his main force were nearing Crooked Creek, on the outskirts of the army camp. Two of his scouts appeared, telling him that there were columns of soldiers approaching from the right.

The Shawnee Chief was dismayed. It meant that they could not carry out their war plan to surround the encampment before the white men became aware of their presence.

Instead, the warriors would be forced to begin the fight in the middle of the forest. Because the Ohio and Kanawha were on either side of the campsite, they could not use their standard tactics of encircling their enemy before attacking, which put the Shawnee army at a disadvantage.

Realizing he had no alternative, Cornstalk sent a large number of his best warriors forward, telling them to hide in the bushes and ambush the rapidly approaching soldiers. When the first of the militiamen came into rifle range of the Indians, a few gunshots rang out, and were soon followed by hundreds more.

The troops were taken completely by surprise by the heavy barrage of bullets, which gave their enemy time to reload and fire again. The frontiersmen then reacted to the assault in the way that they had become accustomed to fighting on the border. They broke rank and fanned out, taking cover in the forest and using trees, logs and brush as cover.

Commanders Lewis and Fleming tried to encourage their men to form into a line across the battle area, but while doing so they exposed themselves to a deadly barrage of gunfire from the Indians. Charles Lewis had worn the bright red jacket from his British uniform into the foray, which made him an easy target for the braves. He made no attempt to take cover when the fighting started. Instead, he stood in the open, urging his men to reform into columns. Within a few minutes of the onslaught of the attack, Lewis was shot. He calmly told his soldiers, "I am hit, but you go on and be brave." Then he made his way back to the encampment. Hearing that Charles was wounded, Colonel Lewis hurried to his brother's side in the officer's tent.

"Charles," Lewis exclaimed, "I expected something fatal would befall you."

"It is the fate of war," Charles answered, and a few moments later he died.

Colonel Fleming was also hit in the opening fire of the battle. He was shot twice in the arm, but continued to fight.

"Don't lose an inch of ground!" he called to his troops.

A third bullet tore through Fleming's chest, knocking him down. As he was carried from the field, Fleming realized that a portion of his lung was protruding from his chest wound, and he calmly pushed it back into his body.

Many of the militia captains were also killed in the first volley of fire from the Indians, including Wilson, Dickenson, Skidmore and Buford. This left a large portion of the army without leadership. Captain Stuart survived, and saw that even though the border militia had no knowledge of the use of discipline or military order, they were well skilled in their own manner of warfare, and began exchanging fire with Cornstalk's warriors from behind the protection of the trees.

Thomas and William, who had been at the front of the Botetourt column, had become separated when the fighting began.

Thomas took cover behind a large tree and was firing with deadly accuracy into the enemy forces. He refused to retreat as Cornstalk's men slowly advanced, and called out to the other frontiersmen around him to stand their ground.

When the first of the wounded soldiers returned to camp and informed Colonel Lewis that the assault was not a skirmish but a full blown attack, he immediately sent reinforcements to the front. Their arrival bolstered the beleaguered militia, and stopped any further advance on the part of the Indians.

By nine o'clock, Chief Cornstalk knew that his original plan for trapping the Southern Army had failed. In most situations he would have signaled his men to fall back, but that was not an option in the present battle. Instead, he told the warriors that they could not retreat and must continue to attack the colonial forces.

Obeying his instructions, the braves came out from behind their cover and openly confronted the militiamen, taking them completely by surprise. With upraised tomahawks and war clubs, the hideously painted Indians rushed towards the colonial army. After a moment, the equally fierce border men emerged from the cover of the forest and engaged their foes in hand to hand combat.

Never before or since has such a battle taken place on the frontier. Men shot each other at point blank range, blowing huge holes in one another. One ferocious native ran directly at Thomas McClung, who cooly stood his ground and shot the man when they were no less than two feet apart.

Thinking he was safe for the moment, Thomas pushed his bloody adversary out of his way, only to find a second warrior directly behind the first, brandishing an upraised war club. Having no time to reload, Thomas struck the Indian across the face with the butt of his rifle, then wrenched the war club from his grasp and knocked the brave to the ground with it, crushing the skull of the savage with one mighty blow.

Taking a moment to look around, Thomas beheld a scene that looked more like a battle of gladiators than a military engagement. Everywhere, soldiers and Indians were attacking one another with knives, tomahawks, bayonets and war clubs. Men of both armies were lying on the ground with grievous wounds, moaning and begging for help.

The air was filled with the smoke of many guns, and with the shrill war cries of the Shawnee braves. Like a scene from some nightmarish hell, it was almost more than Thomas could comprehend.

Shaking his head to clear the smoke from his eyes, Thomas joined the slow advance of the militia as Cornstalk and his men were pushed back toward the small ridge which they had come over that morning. By noon the Indians had been forced to retreat over a mile, and were firmly entrenched on the top of the heavily wooded embankment. The Southern Army had suffered heavy casualties during the six hour battle, and the men were content to hold the ground they had taken, rather than make another attack on the Indians.

During the lull in the fighting, Thomas managed to find William. Miraculously, neither of the men had been seriously wounded during the deadly encounter. Vowing to stay together for the remainder of the conflict, the brothers slowly advanced to the very edge of the enemy line. Runners from the camp brought food and ammunition to the soldiers on the front, and they ate a hasty meal of bread and meat.

As the afternoon wore on, Cornstalk feared that the battle had been lost. His only hope was to try and hold the ridge until nightfall, when his braves could attempt to slip unseen through the forest and gain entry to the camp, where they could massacre the remaining soldiers.

After a brief reprieve, the soldiers tried to make their way up the hill and force the Indians into another retreat. Their anger at the deaths of so many of their fellow frontiersmen had left them fearless and determined to take the ridge. But no matter how many times they pressed forward, the warriors forced them back into the valley.

Finally Colonel Lewis, not wanting to let the battle continue through the night, sent for the best riflemen from the militia, and presented them with a daring mission. They were ordered to travel from the front lines to the point where the two rivers met, and then proceed under the cover of the bank of the Kanawha to the mouth of Crooked Creek.

Once there, the men could follow the bed of the creek to a portion of the cliff that rose up directly behind the ridge where the Indians were entrenched. In that area the wall of the cliff had eroded, and it might be possible for the riflemen to climb to the top and ascend to high ground, which would allow them to lay down a destructive fire on the Indians below.

Thomas and William, both renowned for their skill with the carbine rifle, were among the first men to be chosen for the dangerous maneuver. They, and twenty other sharp shooters, set out at once.

In an hour the men reached the base of the cliff. It took another hour for them to reach an outcrop that rose 100 yards above the ridge where four hundred of Cornstalk's best men had barricaded themselves, repelling every advance the militia made against them, wounding and killing many soldiers in the process.

Immediately, the riflemen scattered along the edge of the cliff, seeking out good vantage points from which to target the enemy below. Thomas and William situated themselves about fifty yards from one another. Watching for the tell tale puff of smoke that rose whenever one of the braves fired a shot, the frontiersmen began pouring a deadly volley of lead into the trees below.

Just before nightfall, Thomas watched as a resolute group of militia men fought their way from the forest floor to the top of the hill that the Indians held. No amount of gunfire from the braves deterred them, even though many of the men were felled in the steady barrage of lead balls and arrows that rained down on them as they forged their way up the mountain.

At last, the soldiers scrambled onto level ground and took shelter behind a huge log at the edge of the forest, and quickly began firing on the braves who had taken cover in the trees a short distance in front of them.

Before long, it seemed that the militia had gotten the upper hand, as the Indians slowly began to fall back. But from his position above the ridge, Thomas could see what his compatriots below could not. A band of about twenty savages was moving up behind them, led by the Shawnee Shaman who carried their scared beeson.

Thomas motioned for William to join him, and pointed out the situation below. Because of the din of battle, there was no way to warn the troops of the danger that was rapidly approaching them from the rear. Only a few of the border men who had climbed the ridge were still able to fight, and none would survive if the sneak attack succeeded.

Thomas opened his cartridge bag and calmly loaded his Pennsylvania rifle. When he was done, he turned and handed the remainder of his powder and ammunition to William.

"Here, take this. You were always a better shot than me anyway," he said.

Then, flashing his brother a grin, Thomas climbed over the side of the cliff and began sliding down the steep incline toward the small ridge. About ten feet before he reached the floor of the cliff, Thomas came to a stand of trees which had grown out in a precarious horizontal position on the side of the mountain. He carefully eased his way through the swaying branches until he was directly above the band of warriors that were almost within range of the unsuspecting militiamen.

Voicing a bone chilling scream that was not unlike the war cry of the Shawnee, Thomas dropped into the middle of the startled Indians. Turning his gun on the closest brave, Thomas shot him in the heart, then shoving him out of the way, he used his bayonet to stab the warrior next to him.

Hearing the confrontation behind them, the soldiers turned and began firing into the oncoming war party. From the cliff above, William shot twice in rapid succession, and two of the braves attacking Thomas crumpled onto the ground.

Three more of the Indians were downed by the rifles of the militia men, leaving Thomas engaged in a fierce battle with four warriors. In spite of a gunshot to his back and the many tomahawk and war club blows that rained down on him from his enemies, Thomas kept his footing and, fighting with a terrible intensity, killed two of the warriors with his tomahawk and wounded the other two so severely that they were unable to rise from the ground.

The grateful soldiers gathered around the mortally wounded frontiersman, and helped him back to the shelter of the fallen tree, where Thomas allowed himself to sink to the ground. It was obvious to the militiamen that Thomas could not recover from his terrible wounds.

Henry Dickenson was one of the soldiers that McClung had rescued, and the young man handed his water bag to his friend. Thomas drank thirstily from the deerskin and gratefully handed it back to Henry.

William had descended the cliff wall and he ran toward the group surrounding the fallen soldier. Giving his brother a weak smile, Thomas motioned for the knife that was hanging from William's belt.

Removing the knife from its sheath, William placed it in his brother's hand and helped him close his fingers around the handle. Painfully, Thomas raised the blade to his head and sheared off his queue with one stroke.

"For Nancy," Thomas whispered weakly to William, handing him the heavy length of black hair. "Tell her I love her. Tell her I will always be with her."

William promised, and took the queue, folding it carefully and placing it in the cartridge bag Thomas had left with him on the cliff. Satisfied, Thomas nodded his thanks to William. Then the frontiersman closed his eyes, and a moment later his head dropped onto his chest.

****

The Southern Commander's strategy had worked flawlessly. Not only did the Indians suffer many casualties from the sharp shooters on the cliff, they also believed that the soldiers firing down on them were reinforcements from the Northern Army, which meant they were now outnumbered almost two to one.

The remainder of Cornstalk's men quickly retreated, leaving behind twenty-three guns, twenty-seven tomahawks, eighty blankets and a large number of animal skins, war clubs, powder horns and cartridge bags on the battlefield as they fled.

Silently, the defeated braves slipped through the forest to where their rafts were hidden, and made their way across the Ohio River. Reaching the northern shore, they traveled on foot through the wilderness to the Indian villages on the Pickaway Plains.

Once they entered Shawnee Town, Cornstalk held a council meeting with all of the Chiefs of the tribes so that they could decide what should be done.

"What will you do now?" he asked them. No one replied.

"The Big Knife (the Northern Army) is coming on us, and we shall all be killed. Now you must fight or we are all undone." There was only silence in the council room.

Cornstalk said angrily, "Let us then kill all our women and children and go and fight till we die."

Still, no one would speak. Finally, Cornstalk stood up and struck the center post in the council house with his war tomahawk.

"I will go and make peace," he said at last, and all the council members agreed.

Runners were sent from the village to meet Lord Dunmore and inform him that the tribes wanted to make peace, giving the Governor a great victory. None of the soldiers under his command had fired a single shot during the conflict.

The Northern Army halted on the Pickaway Plains, at a location the men named Camp Charlotte in honor of Lord Dunmore's wife. Dunmore sent his scouts to summon the leader of every tribe to a meeting.

All of the great Chiefs were present at the convention, and signed a treaty that was called The Terms of Our Reconciliation. In the document, the Indian Nations agreed to the following terms:

1. To give up, without reserve, all the prisoners ever taken by them in war with the white people; and in the future to never again wage war against the frontier colonies of Virginia.

2. To give up all negroes taken by them from white people since the last war; and to pay for all property destroyed by them.

3. To surrender all horses and other valuable effects which they had taken from the white people since the last war.

4. To no more in the future ever hunt on or visit the south side of the Ohio River, except for the purpose of trading with the white people.

5. To no more molest boats of white people,

while they were descending or ascending the Ohio River.

6. To agree to such regulations for trade with the white people as should hereafter be dictated by the King's instruction.

7. To deliver up hostages as a guarantee for the faithful compliance with the terms of the treaty; to be kept by the whites until they were convinced of the sincerity on the part of the Indians to adhere to all of the terms of these articles.

8. To have from the Governor a guarantee that no white people should be permitted to hunt on the northern, or the Indian side of the Ohio River.

9. To meet at Pittsburgh the next spring and enter into a supplemental treaty by which the terms of the treaty at 'Camp Charlotte' should be ratified and fully confirmed.

In return for signing the treaty, Lord Dunmore gave the Indians his word that they would now have the friendship, protection and good will of the Virginia Colony.

****

On Tuesday, October 11th, the surviving militiamen at Point Pleasant spent the day either building a rough log structure to house the wounded, or burying the men who had been killed in the battle the day before. Most of the soldiers were buried where they fell, and sometimes multiple bodies were placed in each grave. Many of the dead had been scalped or mutilated by the Indians, and could not be identified.

William, Henry and a few other men from their company oversaw the burial of

Thomas and the other troops who had died on the small ridge. That evening a funeral service was held in the camp, honoring all of those who had fallen in the conflict.

The company records showed that eighty-one soldiers had been killed during the battle. One hundred and forty additional men were listed as having been wounded, but eventually recovered.

There was no way of knowing exactly how many Indians had died during the fight. Various accountings by the soldiers made it seem likely that as many as three hundred had been killed.

A large number of the fallen warriors were carried away when the defeated braves retreated, but even more were left on the battlefield. They were not buried, but left on the ground until they decomposed or were ravaged by wolves and bears and the other carnivores of the forest.

The Southern Army remained at Point Pleasant until the end of October. It was necessary to wait for the wounded men to heal and for supplies to arrive so they could make the long march back to Camp Union, and from there back to their homes.

Because of the delay, it was not until late November that William McClung and Henry Dickenson rode into the clearing where Thomas and Nancy McClung's log home stood. The day was chilly, and smoke rose lazily from the stone chimney that encompassed one side of the cabin.

Henry seemed uneasy, and told William that he thought it would be best if he did not stay. Asking William to tell Nancy that she could call on him if she ever needed help, he and William shook hands, and Henry turned his horse and rode away.

William dismounted, and loosed his brother's deerskin pouch from his saddle horn. He started toward the cabin, but he had only gone a short distance when Nancy McClung stepped outside, closing the door behind her.

"I know Thomas is dead," she said quietly, pushing the hair back from her face. "It was over a month ago when, just before dark, his wolf began to howl. The beast howled all that night, and in the morning when I got up, it was gone. I knew then that Thomas never coming home," Nancy finished, looking sadly up at William.

"What happened to him? And where did you bury him?" she forlornly asked the frontiersman.

William led Nancy into the cabin, and pulled a chair close to the fireplace for her. He told her what had taken place at Point Pleasant, and how Thomas had died saving the lives of many other soldiers. William looked around the room, where his brother's children stood listening solemnly to his story, and told them that their father was a hero. Then he asked them to go up to the loft so he could speak with their mother alone.

When they had gone, William handed Nancy the leather pouch she had made for Thomas. Gently, he told her to open it.

Nancy reached into the bag and slowly removed the long black queue of hair, pressing it against her cheek. William repeated the message that Thomas had sent her, and Nancy began to cry softly.

"Thank you for this, and for his last

words," Nancy said tearfully. "I will treasure them, and when each of the children leaves home, I will send a lock of their father's hair with them. That way he will never be forgotten."

****

William made the remainder of the trip to Williamsburg alone. He was tired, and saddened at the loss of his brother. Still, his heart brightened when the blockhouse where Abigail and his sons waited for him came into view.

A heavy snow was falling, which muffled the sound of his approach, and it was not until William had thrown open the door that his family was aware he had come home. Abigail gasped, and she and his three boys, who seemed to have grown much bigger during his absence, rushed to greet him, covering him with kisses. Happy and excited, everyone seemed to be talking at once.

William had expected to find his father and mother still at the blockhouse, but they had departed a few weeks earlier, after hearing that a peace treaty had been signed. Abigail said that they wanted to make it back to Lexington before the weather turned bad.

Still, Abigail told William , there was a new family member waiting to meet him. She had given birth several weeks earlier than expected, and now she presented the baby, the couple's first daughter, to her husband.

Abigail had named the child Catherine, after the grandmother who had raised her when her own mother died.

Abigail had only been four at the time, and her father, Joseph Carpenter, could not care for the little girl on his own. Instead, he brought the child to her grandparents, the Dickensons, who lived in Rockbridge County, and they agreed to take her in.

William cradled the sleeping infant in his arms, whispering "Well, Miss Catherine McClung, you are most welcome here. I intend to see that you have a good life."

"To live well and to live free," William thought to himself, "that is what Thomas and the other soldiers at Point Pleasant died fighting for, and that is the legacy that they will be remembered for."

****

The frontiersmen who fought at the

Battle of Point Pleasant returned home to learn that the Continental Congress had issued a Declaration of Colonial Rights, and had voted to create a permanent league of the thirteen Colonies. It was clear to everyone in America that it was only a matter of time before there would be open rebellion against England. The colonial militia left no doubt as to whom they would support.

A few months after the battle, the survivors of Point Pleasant published a joint notice in the Virginia Gazette Newspaper, which became known as The Fort Gower Resolves. It read:

"We have lived about three months in the woods without any intelligence from Boston, or from the delegates at Philadelphia. If there is to be a war with Britain, the Americans will have an army.

That we are a respectable body is certain when it is considered that we can live weeks without bread or salt, that we can sleep in the open air without any covering but that of the canopy of heaven, and that our men can march and shoot with any in the known world. We resolve that we will exert every power within us for the defense of American Liberty."

APPENDIX

THE BATTLE OF POINT PLEASANT

On October 10, 1774, six months before the 'shots heard round the world' were fired at Lexington and Concord, over one thousand rugged colonial militiamen, under the command of Colonel Andrew Lewis, met and defeated the combined forces of the Indian Nations at the confluence of the Ohio and Great Kanawha Rivers. If the Indians had claimed a victory, an alliance between them and the British may have developed during the upcoming Revolutionary War, and weakened the position of the colonists.

The bodies of many of the men who were killed during the battle were buried at 'The Magazine' in Point Pleasant. But 46 soldiers were buried where they fell on the battlefield, and for over two hundred years, they were forgotten by the Nation.

Eventually, the bodies of the men who had been buried on the battlefield were discovered. Using the top forensic scientists and genealogists in the country, the remains of 25 of the men were positively identified, and the other 21 were listed as unknown.

On November 1, 1991, the United States Congress officially voted to recognize those men as Unheralded Patriots, and the facts of their death were entered into the 102nd Congressional Records.

Visit the Thomas McClung website at:
thomasmcclungatpointpleasant.com

Congressional Record
102nd Congress (1991-1992)

BATTLE OF POINT PLEASANT--A CLAIM FOR UNHERALDED PATRIOTS (Senate - November 01, 1991)

[Page: S15798]

Mr. BYRD. Mr. President, I ask my colleagues to join me today in remembering those whom many believe to be the first military veterans in our Nation's history. I am speaking of the militiamen of the Battle of Point Pleasant, a battle waged in my home State of West Virginia--at that time, Virginia--and officially recognized in 1908 by the 60th Congress as the First Battle of the Revolutionary War.

On October 10, 1774--6 months before the `shots heard 'round the world' were fired at Lexington and Concord--800 rugged colonial militiamen, under the command of Col. Andrew Lewis, met and defeated 1,000 Shawnee Indians commanded by Chief Cornstalk at the confluence of the Ohio and Great Kanawha Rivers. If the Shawnees had claimed victory, an alliance with the British may have developed and weakened the position of the colonists. However, the colonists' defeat of the Shawnees demonstrated their military potential and strengthened their stance of independence from official British colonial policy.

The battle and the subsequent peace treaty with the Indians brought relative peace to the Ohio frontier for several years and opened the way for further westward movement by American settlers into the Midwest. But most importantly, it freed the American patriots from having to fear a rearguard Indian attack on the Virginia frontier as the rebellious colonies struggled for their liberty against the King's soldiers during the Revolutionary War.

At the Battle of Point Pleasant, our forefathers took a bold and courageous step toward securing freedom and asserting their independence. The service of these militiamen was a true pledge of allegiance to liberty and self-government and I take pride in honoring the forgotten men who helped shape the destiny of our Nation.

I ask unanimous consent that the list of names of those who fell in battle and were buried at `the Point' on October 11, 1774, be printed in the Record.

There being no objection, the list was ordered to be printed in theRecord,as follows:

Names for Temporary Grave Markers

1. Charles Lewis, Colonel, Army of Virginia, American Revolution, March 11, 1736-October 10, 1774.
2. John Field, Sr., Colonel, Army of Virginia, American Revolution, 1720-October 10, 1774.
3. Thomas Buford, Captain, Army of Virginia, American Revolution, 1736-October 17, 1774.
4. Robert McClanahan, Captain, Army of Virginia, American Revolution, c. 1748-50-October 10, 1774.
5. John Murray, Captain, Army of Virginia, American Revolution, ------ -October 10, 1774.
6. James Ward, Captain, Army of Virginia, American Revolution, c. 1729-October 10, 1774.
7. Samuel Wilson, Captain, Army of Virginia, American Revolution, 1730-October 10, 1774.
8. Hugh Allen, Lieutenant, Army of Virginia, American Revolution, c. 1745-October 10, 1774.
9. Matthew Bracken, Lieutenant, Army of Virginia, American Revolution, ------ -October 10, 1774.
10. Edward Goldman, Lieutenant, Army of Virginia, American Revolution, ------ -October 17, 1774.
11. Jonathan Cundiff, Ensign, Army of Virginia, American Revolution, ------ -October 10, 1774.
12. George Cameron, Private, Army of Virginia, American Revolution, ------ -October 10, 1774.
13. Richard Trotter, Sergeant, Army of Virginia, American Revolution, c. 1738-October 10, 1774.
14. Samuel Croley, Private, Army of Virginia, American Revolution, ------ -October 10, 1774.
15. John Dinwiddie, Private, Army of Virginia, American Revolution, ------ -October 10, 1774.
16. Joseph Hughey, Private, Army of Virginia, American Revolution, ------ -October 10, 1774.
17. Thomas McClung, Private, Army of Virginia, American Revolution, c. 1728-October 10, 1774.
18. James Mooney, Private, Army of Virginia, American Revolution, ------ -October 10, 1774.
19. Hugh O'Gullion, Private, Army of Virginia, American Revolution, ------ -October 10, 1774.
20. William Stephen, Private, Army of Virginia, American Revolution, c. 1760-October 10, 1774.
21. Isaac Van Bibber, Private, Army of Virginia, American Revolution, p. 1725-October 10, 1774.
22. David White, Private, Army of Virginia, American Revolution, ------ -October 10, 1774.
23. Marck Williams, Private, Army of Virginia, American Revolution, ------ -October 10, 1774.
24. David Kincaid, Private, Army of Virginia, American Revolution, ------ -October 10, 1774.
25. John Frogg, Jr., Captain/Sutler, Army of Virginia, American Revolution, May 26, 1745-October 10, 1774.
26. Twenty-one whose names are unknown, Privates, Army of Virginia, American Revolution, -October 10, 1774.

Congressional Record for Thomas McClung

THOMAS McCLUNG

Thomas McClung was born in 1728, to John and Rebecca Stuart McClung. He married Nancy Black. They lived on in Greenbrier County. Thomas McClung was killed at the Battle of Point Pleasant on October 10, 1774, and was buried on the battlefield. Many sources, including the U.S. Congress and the Sons of the American Revolution, have provided numerous records that prove Thomas McClung died at Point Pleasant. These include verified McClung family Bible records, sworn statement of Private Henry Dickenson, who was a friend of Thomas McClung, and testified that he had witnessed his death and burial on the battlefield at Point Pleasant on October 10, 1774.

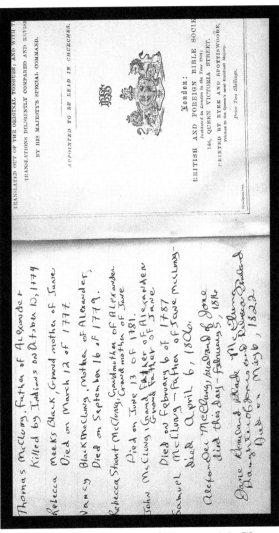

Bible records of death of Thomas McClung

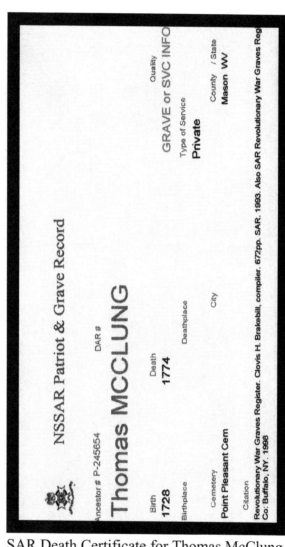

SAR Death Certificate for Thomas McClung

Thomas McClung
in the U.S., Sons of the American Revolution Membership Applications, 1889-1970

Name:	Thomas McClung
Birth Date:	1728
Death Date:	10 Oct 1774
SAR Membership:	72358
Role:	Ancestor
Application Date:	9 Mar 1952
Father:	John McClung
Mother:	Rebecca Stuart
Spouse:	Nancy Black
Children:	John McClung

Source Information

Ancestry.com. *U.S., Sons of the American Revolution Membership Applications, 1889-1970* [database on-line]. Provo, UT, USA: Ancestry.com Operations, Inc., 2011.

Original data: *Sons of the American Revolution Membership Applications, 1889-1970.* Louisville, Kentucky: National Society of the Sons of the American Revolution. Microfilm, 508 rolls.

National Society, Sons of the American Revolution

Description

This database contains applications for membership in the National Society of the Sons of the American Revolution approved between 1889 and 31 December 1970. These records can be an excellent source for names, dates, locations, and family relationships. Learn more...

© 2016, Ancestry.com

SAR Patriot Thomas McClung

Nancy Black
in the U.S., Sons of the American Revolution Membership Applications, 1889-1970

Name:	Nancy Black
SAR Membership:	62349
Role:	Ancestor
Application Date:	25 May 1943
Spouse:	Thomas McClung
Children:	John McClung

Source Citation
Volume: 312

Source Information
Ancestry.com. *U.S., Sons of the American Revolution Membership Applications, 1889-1970* [database on-line]. Provo, UT, USA: Ancestry.com Operations, Inc., 2011.

Original data: *Sons of the American Revolution Membership Applications, 1889-1970*. Louisville, Kentucky: National Society of the Sons of the American Revolution. Microfilm, 508 rolls.

National Society, Sons of the American Revolution

Description
This database contains applications for membership in the National Society of the Sons of the American Revolution approved between 1889 and 31 December 1970. These records can be an excellent source for names, dates, locations, and family relationships. Learn more...

© 2016, Ancestry.com

SAR Patriot Nancy Black McClung

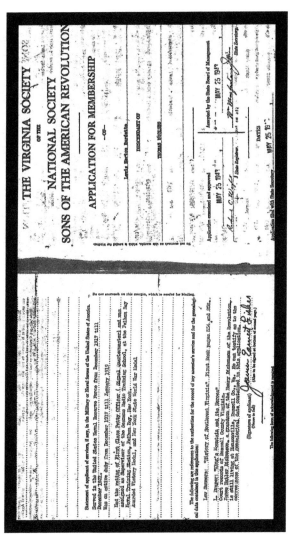

Henry Dickenson Battle of PP Witness

Thomas MCCLUNG P-245654 VA
1728 1774

NSSAR Patriot Biography

Thomas McClung was born in 1728. He was a pioneer and frontiersman on the Virginia border. He married Nancy Black. In 1774, he fought at the Battle of Point Pleasant, which has been named by the US Congress as the first battle of the Revolutionary War. Thomas was killed during the battle, and his body, along with those of several other men, was buried on the site of the conflict. Because these men were not transported to the Cemetery at Point Pleasant with the other casualties, there names were not included on the monument there, and there was some controversy as to whether they did die at the battle.

After much genealogical research, however, it was proven that these unheralded patriots did indeed die in the battle and the Congress of the US unanimously voted to accept the evidence and entered into the 102 Congressional Record (1991-1992) that Pvt. Thomas McClung and the other men did die in the battle and were buried on the battle field.

BATTLE OF POINT PLEASANT–A CLAIM FOR UNHERALDED PATRIOTS (Senate - November 01, 1991) [Page: S15798]

Mr. BYRD. Mr. President, I ask my colleagues to join me today in remembering those whom many believe to be the first military veterans in our Nation's history. I am speaking of the militiamen of the Battle of Point Pleasant, a battle waged in my home State of West Virginia–at that time, Virginia–and officially recognized in 1908 by the 60th Congress as the First Battle of the Revolutionary War.

On October 10, 1774–6 months before the 'shots heard 'round the world' were fired at Lexington and Concord–800 rugged colonial militiamen, under the command of Col. Andrew Lewis, met and defeated 1,000 Shawnee Indians commanded by Chief Cornstalk at the confluence of the Ohio and Great Kanawha Rivers. If the Shawnees had claimed victory, an alliance with the British may have developed and weakened the position of the colonists. However, the colonists' defeat of the Shawnees demonstrated their military potential and strengthened their stance of independence from official British colonial policy.
The battle and the subsequent peace treaty with the Indians brought relative peace to the Ohio frontier for several years and opened the way for further westward movement by American settlers into the Midwest. But most importantly, it freed the American patriots from having to fear a rearguard Indian attack on the Virginia frontier as the rebellious colonies struggled for their liberty against the King's soldiers during the Revolutionary War.

At the Battle of Point Pleasant, our forefathers took a bold and courageous step toward securing freedom and asserting their independence. The service of these militiamen was a true pledge of allegiance to liberty and self-government and I take pride in honoring the forgotten men who helped shape the destiny of our Nation.

I ask unanimous consent that the list of names of those who fell in battle and were buried at 'the Point' on October 11, 1774, be printed in the Record.
There being no objection, the list was ordered to be printed in the Record, as follows:

Names for Temporary Grave Markers

1. Charles Lewis, Colonel, Army of Virginia, American Revolution, March 11, 1736-October 10, 1774.
2. John Field, Sr., Colonel, Army of Virginia, American Revolution, 1720-October 10, 1774.
3. Thomas Buford, Captain, Army of Virginia, American Revolution, 1736-October 17, 1774.
4. Robert McClanahan, Captain, Army of Virginia, American Revolution, c. 1748-50-October 10, 1774.
5. John Murray, Captain, Army of Virginia, American Revolution, ----- -October 10, 1774.
6. James Ward, Captain, Army of Virginia, American Revolution, c. 1729-October 10, 1774.
7. Samuel Wilson, Captain, Army of Virginia, American Revolution, 1730-October 10, 1774.
8. Hugh Allen, Lieutenant, Army of Virginia, American Revolution, c. 1745-October 10, 1774.
9. Matthew Bracken, Lieutenant, Army of Virginia, American Revolution, ----- -October 10, 1774.
10. Edward Goldman, Lieutenant, Army of Virginia, American Revolution, ----- -October 17, 1774.
11. Jonathan Cundiff, Ensign, Army of Virginia, American Revolution, ----- -October 10, 1774.
12. George Cameron, Private, Army of Virginia, American Revolution, ----- -October 10, 1774.
13. Richard Trotter, Sergeant, Army of Virginia, American Revolution, c. 1738-October 10, 1774.
14. Samuel Croley, Private, Army of Virginia, American Revolution, ----- -October 10, 1774.
15. John Dinwiddie, Private, Army of Virginia, American Revolution, ----- -October 10, 1774.
16. Joseph Hughey, Private, Army of Virginia, American Revolution, ----- -October 10, 1774.
17. Thomas McClung, Private, Army of Virginia, American Revolution, c. 1728-October 10, 1774.
18. James Mooney, Private, Army of Virginia, American Revolution, ----- -October 10, 1774.
19. Hugh O'Gullion, Private, Army of Virginia, American Revolution, ----- -October 10, 1774.
20. William Stephen, Private, Army of Virginia, American Revolution, c. 1780-October 10, 1774.
21. Isaac Van Bibber, Private, Army of Virginia, American Revolution, p. 1725-October 10, 1774.
22. David White, Private, Army of Virginia, American Revolution, ----- -October 10, 1774.
23. Marck Williams, Private, Army of Virginia, American Revolution, ----- -October 10, 1774.
24. David Kincaid, Private, Army of Virginia, American Revolution, ----- -October 10, 1774.
25. John Frogg, Jr., Captain/Sutler, Army of Virginia, American Revolution, May 26, 1745-October 10, 1774.
26. Twenty-one whose names are unknown, Privates, Army of Virginia, American Revolution, ----- -October 10, 1774.

SAR Patriot Biography of Thomas McClung

RESOURCES

Richmond, Nancy., *William McClung-Appalachian Frontiersman,* Charleston, SC, CreateSpace Publishing., 2013.

Lewis, Virgil A., *History of the Battle of Point Pleasant.,.* Charleston, WV., The Tribune Printing Company, 1909.

Winkler, John F. and Dennis, Peter., *Point Pleasant 1774: Prelude to the American Revolution.,* Osprey Publishing., 2014.

Fleming, William, *Journal and Orderly Book, Documentary History of Dunmore's War.*, The National Historic Society., printed in Wisconsin. 1981.

Stuart, John., *Memoirs of the Indian Wars and Other Occurrences.,* reprinted by McClain Print Company, 1971.

CPSIA information can be obtained
at www.ICGtesting.com
Printed in the USA
LVHW081101300320
651625LV00019B/1447